I0484156

The Disruption Code

A Guide to Cracking the Innovation Mystery

Julie Beckers

Copyright © 2015 Julie Beckers

All rights reserved.

ISBN-10:1511637447
ISBN-13:978-1511637442

DEDICATION

For my two wonderful children Blair and Lana for
making me who I am today and for always
challenging the status quo. They are wonderful
disrupters.

CONTENTS

ACKNOWLEDGMENTS

Books don't just happen on their own they are the culmination of many years of research and experience and have the input and support of many people to make them happen. I would like to thank my amazing friends especially Wesley who is a wonderful wordsmith himself, and my family for supporting me through the process and for their tireless reviewing and editing. A big thank you must also go to Phillip Dannels for the wonderful work he did on the creation of the cover and Kon Iatrou for his fantastic work on my photos. I am extremely grateful to the many people who have taught me a great number of things, and the people who have encouraged my creativity and finally, the great writers whose footsteps I followed on my journey through Paris, for providing me with the inspiration to finally author my own book.

INTRODUCTION

Do you find your business unable to keep up with its competitors? Are you clueless about how to create innovative products and services?

The Disruption Code will enable you to unlock the secrets to leaping ahead of your competitors and help you and your team to unlock the right problems and create solutions for you to provide innovative products and services. You will learn how to keep up with constant change and discover the secrets to making innovation part of your business' DNA and master business development with the tools of Design Thinking coupled with modern and traditional tools of business. The Disruption Code will start you off with your own repertoire of concepts and tools to help you create the platforms for innovation to transform your business.

Authors write the books they need. After over two decades of being a designer of disruptive business and service delivery models, and on a mission to make sure that businesses can think as if there is no box, along with adapting to an ever-changing world, this book has evolved to give you an easy guide to the ingredients of creating the platform for incremental and disruptive innovation. Each chapter provides you with tips on how to use the tools of Design Thinking to create the right environment for innovation in your business. My hope is that this book becomes a well-worn friend of yours.

1 IN THE BEGINNING THERE WAS DISRUPTION AND CHANGE

"The only way to make sense out of change is to plunge into it, move with it, and join the dance".

Alan Watts

A World of Constant Change

Like many people I can remember carrying a mobile phone that resembled a brick around in my handbag. I also remember before that, having to go to a phone box to call my friends, and no, it wasn't a 'Tardis' (although there was always the hope of meeting up with 'Superman'). Now I carry my phone, which doubles as a mini computer, around in my back pocket. Heaven forbid I should leave it on my bedside table on my way out the door though, as phone boxes are now extremely few and far between! And that's not to mention the social media withdrawals that one experiences without contact with my networks on Facebook®, LinkedIn®, Instagram®, Google+®, Twitter® or the like. I don't actually need to use the phone function on my phone anymore, and my text messages come straight through to my computer.

Many of us remember having to carry our luggage on our backs when we travelled and the consequential visits to the chiropractor for doing so. Now we have wheels on our luggage and travel on planes more than we do on buses and trains. We now book our accommodation through the sharing economy on Airbnb®, our rides on Uber®, and our flights via apps on our phones. Well, that's if we've remembered to take our phones with us. As consumers we now have so much choice that sometimes it's so very hard to choose.

Now, you may very well be saying this woman is 'old'. I might be old, but I'm not *that* old. These changes have happened recently and very, very QUICKLY. My guess is that it won't be long before we will be 3D printing our own custom luggage, the clothing inside and perhaps even travelling in a 3D printed plane. These are just a few examples of products and industries that have been disrupted. Can you think of some yourself?

In today's contemporary world the rate of change and innovation is so rapid that a new and very real problem has emerged for businesses – staying up to date and relevant! Today's 'business as usual' **is** change.

Technological disruptive innovations like the jet plane, satellite communication and the Internet have allowed businesses to expand across national borders and become global economic players. For businesses operating within what has now become a global marketplace, this rate of change is of particular concern. So many businesses are here today and gone tomorrow. We are constantly hearing the catch cries of 'innovate or die' or, 'disrupt or be disrupted' and even 'innovate or evaporate'. Indeed, today's businesses operate in an environment where disruption is constant, inevitable, and creativity is abound. New paradigms and products, such as 'Artificial Intelligence' and 'The Internet of Everything', are constantly emerging.

Rapid Technological Change

We are seeing technology change faster than ever before. Not since the Industrial Revolution have we experienced such rapid growth in innovation. The rapid change that is occurring in technology has created a new era in our history. Information Technology is changing our traditional notions of how we operate our businesses. This new "age of technology" brings with it a new set of challenges. The new business imperative is to remain current with the latest technologies and to be ever vigilant about what is happening with changing technologies. If you are a service delivery provider and you under the impression that technological change doesn't apply to you, think again. Technology changes not only bring about new products, they are changing the way we deliver services too. Modern consumers are demanding modern services delivered to them, when and how they want them and now more than ever have the connectedness with the global economy that enables them to connect with services anywhere in the world.

Connectivity a New Era of Connectedness

Our world is in a state of ever-growing connection and innovation. We are seeing new innovations that create our world experience introduced daily. Many of which will ultimately change the way we experience the world.

New connected products are helping us with our daily lives. How would you like your shoes to monitor your workout or get messages from your dryer or a refrigerator that connects to the Internet? Using the networking abilities of the high-speed Internet connections available and increasing speeds of mobile phone technology, you will be able to do exactly that. Sensor technology will connect devices that you haven't even thought of to your wireless devices and your home or indeed your mobile computers.

One of the most interesting uses of the Internet of Things technology is Nike+®, their running shoe has a sensor built right into the shoe. The sensor sends data to your iPod® or iPhone where you can track your run. The app comes with it's own Nike® social network where you can post your data. You can even have the app post "tweets" on Twitter® or update your Facebook® status about your run. Quite an innovative way to track your workouts!

IBM® has been developing its "Smarter Planet" network designed specifically for the Internet of Things technologies. In several cities IBM® has used this technology to deploy congestion management systems. It has seen results with lower emissions and lower traffic volume during normally high traffic volume times.

HP® has also created a similar Internet of Things network called CENSE which stands for Central Nervous System for the Earth. They intend to create networks of sensor devices to pull in data about things like temperature, airflow and sound. Retail, governments, traffic, weather and a host of other possibilities can then use this network of things for a multitude of possible applications.

There is also Internet of Things ideas being tested and used for things like a sticker sensor that can be placed in shop windows, that if you touch your phone to takes you to the shop's website instantly.

Already, there are special data matrix codes made just for smart phone scanning. The growing trend is to have business cards with data matrix codes at the cash register of a shop.

Radio Frequency Identification (RFID) technology will evolve to make it easier to use your smartphone for making purchases. It is amazing what kind of data could be brought to people (and what kind of Big Data could be collected by companies) through their Internet ready devices including their wearable devices. Some researchers are also suggesting that RFID devices will be directly inserted underneath our skin in the near future.

Home automation is certainly an area where Internet of Things technology is being used. From home security systems that work through smart phone apps or through your personal devices and computers to refrigerators that not only give you Internet access, but also order your shopping as your supplies deplete. There are ides that allow your refrigerator to pick up information from any item you store that could be used to monitor nutritional information for that diet you are working on or just to keep a home inventory letting you know when you run out of something.

Your washer and dryer may someday soon let you know by text when your laundry is done. The possibilities of networking your home devices is endless. I just wish they would invent a smoke detector that I can tell, "I just burnt the toast shut up!"

People already enjoy the networking advantages of their Blue-ray players or gaming systems where they can get content directly to their device over the Internet.

The world is growing in the realm of technology so quickly that we can only wonder what the Internet of Things capability will do for us. High-speed Internet connections are a necessity in this electronic age. Home networks will likely be used for more than just connecting your laptop in the near future. It may be connecting your dryer, coffee machine, television, refrigerator, lights or heating too. It will be interesting to see what innovations this technology brings. Is your business Internet of Things and integral connectivity ready?

Disrupt or Be Disrupted

The very existence of new and emerging technologies like 'the Internet of Things' indeed means that businesses need to create an environment for both incremental and disruptive innovation. The notion of "Disrupt or be Disrupted" reminds us that we should aim to be at the forefront of our industries.

Examples of companies and brands that have failed to transform or disrupt and eventually vanished are in abundance. You only need to look at the news or your Twitter® feed each day to see them. Some brands simply go out of fashion. Remember drinking TAB? And whatever happened to Cobbers? Now we go to our fridge or cupboard and take out some new super food or organic something or other that tastes like chaff, but we eat it anyway because it's supposedly good for us.

Companies that are so slow to adapt find that their competition overtakes them. Blockbuster Video®, Kodak® and Compaq® computers are great examples of this. In fact, research shows that for most of the 20th century, the life expectancy of an Standard & Poor's Top 500 company was more than 50 years; now it is 15 years and falling fast. Many companies and brands that are familiar to us today will no longer exist within the next decade. Now that's a scary thought when you are running a business!

Large companies are usually aware of the trends happening in their industry. Where they fall down is that they fail to put the right people or enough resources into looking at new opportunities. For these companies the changing environment creates the imperative for them to realize the opportunities and reinvent themselves accordingly. Will your industry be disrupted? Yes sooner or later it will.

The Imperative for Innovation and Change in the Australian Context

As the Global Financial Crisis (GFC) highlighted, nations are no longer isolated economies. The notion of nation states has indeed now given way to a new global economy – the world without economic borders we all moaned about in the 80's and 90's is here with a vengeance.

Throughout the GFC, Australia's economy remained relatively strong. We continued to experience modest growth in the economy. We were somewhat sheltered from the storm that brought some of the largest economies in the world to their knees. While much of the world was hurting, the Australian economy remained relatively robust without dipping into recession. In fact, there hasn't been a recession here in over 20 years.

Post GFC, however, the Australian economy has slowed. Manufacturing companies are moving overseas, the mining boom has finished and the global economy is picking up speed once more. Australia, now more than ever, needs to be a place of innovation if it is to remain current and compete in the global economy.

Business Model Innovation in Australia

Australia is a clever country. It has a long history of invention dating back many thousands of years with its first people. Let's face it we have invented some amazing things like the Hill's Hoist, the Black Box flight recorder and Internet Wi-Fi as examples. These inventions are just a few of the many things we have invented here.

We are a clever country indeed, but there is one very important thing that we are lagging behind in, and that one big thing is Business Model Disruption. Our corporate business community is stuck in old mindsets, using out-dated models of business, complex business structures and is falling fast behind in the race to compete in the Global economy. There are few examples of disruptive business models the likes of Apple® or Amazon® to be seen in Australia. In other words, Australian industries and their Business Models are ripe for Disruption. Let's hope the clever country remains just that and our companies remain competitive into the future. The very recognition of the rate of change in the world today creates the urgency for Business Model Disruption in Australian businesses, unlike any other time in our history.

A New Discourse for Change

"Keep your friends close and your enemies closer."

Sun Tzu

We know this constant change is happening around us whether we like it or not. While our world has always experienced change, however, the rate of change is speeding up exponentially, so much so that old paradigms of change management and the notions of change adaptation are fast becoming dinosaurs. Change management theories like Kurt Lewin's 1940's three-phase model of "Unfreezing – Transition – Freezing" that take a linear approach to the 'management' of change have become somewhat obsolete in today's world. Indeed, the very notion that change can be 'managed' has become irrelevant. By the time you've put in place change management structures the world has simply passed you by.

Let's face it - change is all about people. Yet it remains that as creatures of habit many of us are very uncomfortable with change. 'We've always done it this way', 'if it's not broke don't fix it', 'We tried that back in 1980 and it didn't work then'. Sound familiar? For some it's difficult to get comfortable with change, but most of us can relate to Sun Tzu's (later attributed to "The Godfather Part II, 1974") quote from his book 'The Art of War' (6th Century BC), "keep your friends close and your enemies closer."

In order to create disruption your business needs to be open to change. If you view change as your ally then "keep your friends close"; if you view change as your foe then "keep your enemies closer". However you view change, you need to become very close and comfortable with it.

The key for businesses, whether for profit or not-for-profit, in a world of constant change is to become a change champion, a game changer, to challenge the status quo and become the disrupter. In other words, disrupt or be disrupted by sharpening your ability to seize new opportunities and identify future trends.

Business Model Disruption

What is Business Model Disruption? When we think about disruption in an industry we often think about a specific product, however very rarely is it the product itself that is the disruption. It's actually business model disruption. So what is business model disruption? The iPod is the most well known example of this. At a time when an oligopoly existed within the music industry, it was seen as a major disruption. The iPod made it possible to carry a whole lot of music around in your pocket. However, the iPod wasn't the only digital music player on the market; there were a heap of MP3 players around at the same time, and it definitely wasn't the first portable music player either (remember the Sony® Walkman?). What was different and disruptive was the business model that Apple® created behind the iPod. The iPod connected to iTunes, which connected to the iTunes music store, where music could be purchased easily and conveniently within a few clicks. No longer did we have to purchase a whole album of music to have our favorite songs. The business model behind the iPod was the digital music business. Apple® enabled its customers to purchase the music they wanted when they wanted it. Apple® did all of this without selling a single CD. Apple's® clever business model disruption carries on today, with the iPhone, iPad and its computer products; all applications link to iTunes or the App Store to enable downloads of not only music, but games, TV shows, movies, apps and a plethora of software applications. The release of Apple® Music this year brings with it a new subscription service where consumers pay by the month to listen to live stream music.

Amazon® also cleverly created their what is now a multi-billion-dollar business through the use of a disruptive business model that would ultimately change worldwide consumer behavior to the demise of many a local bookstore, large and small. Zappos.com® disrupted the shoe store industry by selling shoes online, and the list goes on.

Are you seeing the pattern here? Innovation doesn't only mean new products; it can also be a result of disruption in the business model. Yes Amazon® sold books, but books have been around for centuries, and are definitely not a disruptive product. What Amazon® sold was its service, convenience and more importantly Amazon® sold trust - trust in online purchasing through secure purchasing all from the comfort of your sofa.

Disrupting an established industry or business is fast becoming a type of Business Model in itself. The process of disruption often sneaks up on incumbent companies within an industry. Although these companies may very well be aware of changing technologies within their marketplaces before a disruption occurs, they are often slow to respond due to their traditional business structures. Indeed, responding may also be difficult to manage and so imminent change is often swept under the carpet to deal with later.

To disrupt your Business Model you need to look for gaps or unmet, or often unknown customer needs within current marketplaces and filling those gaps with a new product or service. Every exchange in a business' value chain, and its relationship with customers, staff, owners or community, provides opportunities for disruptive innovation.

But what does it take for businesses to create this type of disruption, get comfortable with change and also develop new and exciting models for business? Here are a few things:

- Agility
- Ideation

- Creativity
- Collaboration
- Customer Co-creation
- Invention
- Iteration
- Rapid Prototyping

And most importantly, fostering a business environment that is conducive to change and creation! Now is the time to disrupt your business model. Okay, no one said this was going to be easy, but you will learn some of the secrets to this in upcoming chapters.

Caught up in the day to day.

As we have seen, it is an exciting time for consumers and business. Yesterday I couldn't buy an Apple Watch®, today I can. Artificial Intelligence is about to disrupt many industries. Invention and reinvention are happening everywhere.

Innovation is, however, easier said than done when we are caught up in the day-to-day running of a business. Business leaders spend their days managing risk, operations, quality, human resources and all the things that go hand in hand with the traditional notion of 'maximizing shareholder value'. As businesses grow bigger and better, they also become increasingly averse to risk. In other words there is tendency for larger companies to avoid risky, costly projects that could result in disruptive innovation. For most managers, their first instinct is to always integrate the innovation process into their current models. This at best may provide slow incremental changes. But by doing so, managers impose overwhelming structures, rules, and an institutionalized 'slowness' on to their team, resulting in a maintenance of the status quo.

The fact that technology will disrupt entrenched business models is no longer news. As business leaders, how we respond to those disruptions is the most important challenge facing businesses today. What will Toyota do in response to the new driverless cars that are about to launch? How will Sony® Music respond to Apple® Music? As a business leader, are you equipped to navigate this new business landscape?

Innovation DNA

Creating a culture that is resilient, flexible and adaptable, thinks not only outside the box but like there is no box, is open to change and ultimately makes disruptive and incremental innovation part of its DNA, can be done and is being done now. Take a look around and you will see that many of the world's most interesting, exciting and profitable companies like Amazon®, Google®, Apple®, Netflix®, Skype®, Fiverr® and Uber® are doing it daily. They have innovation mindsets and disruption at the core of their existence.

The primary source of any innovation in any type of business comes from the minds of its people. By creating a business space that is conducive to disruption and innovation and preparing the minds of leaders and employees, businesses discover and realize new opportunities to create an enduring capacity to innovate. This is where designers can teach business leaders a thing or two through the way they create. This is the notion behind Design Thinking for business. It's also the key to cracking the Disruption Code.

What's Next?

In this chapter, we have looked at the increasing rate of change that the world is experiencing. We have also looked at how as businesses we need to respond to this change or face 'evaporation'. We too have commenced a new discourse for change management. In the next chapter, we look at the first ingredient in cracking the Disruption Code through Design Thinking.

Over to you!

Take some time to think about your own business and how the rate of change may be affecting you. Can you think of any possible ways your industry might be disrupted?

Write down two challenges your business faces in the current climate of change.	
Do you consider your team to be adaptable and flexible to change?	
Do you regularly research your competitors or other industries?	
Would you describe your business as having an open-minded creative mindset?	

2 DISRUPTING THE WORKPLACE

"Learning and innovation go hand in hand. The arrogance of success is to think that what you did yesterday will be sufficient for tomorrow."

William Pollard

Creating the Right Environment for Innovation.

Is your workplace conducive to innovation? Are your leaders open to anything other then the 9 to 5? Does your staff sit at desks all day? Is there a sense of fun in the workplace? Do you have a diverse workplace population?

Before we can even begin to crack the Disruption Code it is important to make sure our workplaces are conducive to creative thinking and change.

Workplaces of the Now and the Future.

The now and the future of how we work is changing and thank goodness for that! The 9 to 5 job is fast becoming a thing of the past. Sitting in a cubicle or office is becoming a thing of the past. Endless hours wasted in traffic is becoming a thing of the past. Contemporary workplaces are becoming collaboration workspaces, commuting is fast becoming a thing of the past, and we are stepping outside the boundaries of the 'norm' in how we engage and retain our staff.

Contemporary workspace

Why are we doing this? Many of you may relate to this story:

I can remember sitting for what seemed like hours in my car on a busy road getting to and from a 9 to 5 place of work. Our CEO, was a traditional thinker with a must be in the office from nine to five policy and old-fashioned ideas around bums on seats. The daily grind of sitting in relentless traffic for 2 hours seemed to me to be the biggest waste of time imaginable, and it was. I am a morning person. Most of my creative ideas come in the morning. I am more productive in the morning. I can achieve much more at

5 am than I can at 5 pm.

I would arrive in the square white box that was my office (my jail for the day), in the morning knowing I would be climbing the walls by 10 am wanting to escape the boring surrounds, the insidious office gossip, the pessimism of the rest of the exec team, the 'I'm so busy' attitudes, the awful office supplied because its cheap coffee, and the air conditioning that was too cold in winter and too hot in summer. (Can someone please invent air-conditioning that somewhat resembles the outside world? Or maybe just make those windows opening? Now that's an idea.) Everyday I would tell myself "keep the optimism up for the sake of the company and your staff".

How difficult it was to create an environment of optimism, empowerment and fun for the staff working for me in the company.

Thinking back I would remember that over the years I had, had the opportunity to create fun and interesting workplaces where my teams could come to work for the experience and achieved greatness. We talked about coming to 'Fun' rather than 'Work'. I have introduced programs like the 'Fish Philosophy' into workplaces. Put up basketball hoops and created chill out spaces for my teams. Time to do it over again? Yes indeed!

With much credit to my amazing team (and with the help of some office plants and funky artwork) together we created a collaborative environment, turned our workplace into a place of fun and consequently, grew and turned that company into a profitable company that increased its market-share by 50%.

A Brave New World

'Times they are a changing', now creating a workplace that is conducive to creativity and collaboration, enables the best from its people and takes into account individual's work styles and peak performance is an imperative of business. Workplaces like this are fast becoming the new 'norm'.

Workers in the past worked the 9 to 5, in a corporate office and used corporate equipment and climbed the corporate ladder. Yesterday's workers were focused on inputs. Tomorrow's workers work anytime, anywhere, use any device, create their own ladder and are focused on outputs. Is your company stuck in yesterday?

Innovative companies like Google®, Ikea®, Facebook®, are doing it and you can too. No matter what industry you are in the benefits of creative workspaces and flexible working arrangements far outweigh any costs involved in their introduction. People want to come to work and they are far more productive when they are at work. Starts up hubs are great examples of people wanting to come together in a creative space to collaborate with others and grow their businesses. Giving people options creates company loyalty and means the best brains actually stay with the company. Creating the space for collaboration brings new ideas and fresh approaches... our customers love it, it enables us to embed innovation mindsets into our company DNA and for those of you reporting to Boards you can work out a return on investment (ROI). Do a search online to see what others are doing. How can you create innovation mindsets in your company through a creative workspace and flexible working conditions?

3 Ways to Improve Innovation Through Diversity.

E Pluribus Unum is Latin for "out of many, one," or "many uniting into one". It is the key to our success, our ability to collaborate... to unite. E Pluribus Unum is also a great vision for today's businesses. In the contemporary workplace, we have a diverse mix of gender, ethnicity, religion and perspectives. We are a mix, and from this mix we can learn to take our best and bring it forward. The world is no longer a melting pot where we all blend, it is now a 'mixed salad' where each component retains it's own identity and adds to the total – "from many, one". The more diverse the greater the salad.

There is true performance power in a diverse workforce in today's workplace because our business world has changed. We have moved from manufacturing to service, from industrial to intellectual, from brawn to brain. As author Seth Godin said, "we used to make food (agrarian society), then we made things (industrial age), now we make ideas" (service economy). Much of our manufacturing has moved offshore and left us with a service economy. Service is an intellectual and thinking environment. In contemporary society, every service is about providing an 'experience'. Therefore, today's employees must think through each service event to maximize the effect on the customer. How an employee thinks is far more important than what they look like.

In contemporary workplaces, we need to hire employees for their talents and thinking; diversity is an added bonus. Gender and religion do not matter. Age or ethnicity does not matter. Thinking matters. The right thinking that drives results may show up in an employee whose age, gender, religion or ethnicity is not one that you expected. It is our role as business leaders to find, hire and encourage the best thinking employees from diverse backgrounds and experiences and unite them into a performance powerhouse. E Pluribus Unum.

Diversity is great for business. It expands our thinking, connects us to our world and encourages great individual contribution. No look at the following ways to create a more diverse workplace with greater opportunity to innovate. Great things happen when employees who do not all look or think the same work side-by-side:

1. Diverse workforces represent the true

population of the country. We have gone global; we communicate minute by minute with the rest of the world. We buy their products; they buy ours. Our workplace must represent our population – mixed and diverse. Our products and services must reflect the markets that are served. Selling to women without a feminine perspective is shortsighted. Selling to others without understanding their language and culture leads to failure. A diverse workforce more fairly represents its customer base so that decisions made at all levels are more appropriate and successful. By 2042 minorities will account for more than half of the Australian population. Nearly sixty percent of university graduates are women. Understanding diverse perspectives allows you to compete globally and more effectively.

How well do you understand your customer population? Does your workforce connect to your customers? Are you open to diverse perspectives, experiences and ideas?

2. When you consider diversity, you have
a greater population to choose from
when searching to hire the "right"
employees. We are in an era of
intellectual workplaces where thinking
matters most. Today we must hire for
talent and that talent is represented by
the "inside" not the "outside" of a
person. We hire thinking – and the
right thinking for a job may show up in
the form of a man or a woman, Greek
or Italian, Muslim or Christian, Old or
Young. When we consider the entire
population of workers to assess the
talents needed in a particular role, we
improve the possibility of finding and
hiring the "right" employee, one who
has the "right" talents, skills and
attitude to be successful in the role.

What is your process to hire employees for
their thinking and talents? How do you
ensure that you consider every qualified
candidate without bias? What is the benefit
to you of having the "right" employee in each
role in your workplace?

3. Diverse workplaces add value, color,

energy and tradition to enable innovation. Diverse workplaces benefit from the mix of cultures, experiences, attitudes and life stories. This adds energy and vibrancy to the workplace; it also forces people who don't necessarily see the world in the same way to learn to work with each other, solve problems together and collaborate for success. Using the power of their mixed backgrounds consistently yields greater responses and greater results.

How do you openly support and celebrate a diverse mix of employees in your workplace? How can you use employee's diverse backgrounds to expand your solutions to problems and business opportunities? How can you encourage employees to appreciate and respect other's differences?

Organizations are learning to celebrate instead of fear, diversity. Diversity offers businesses the ability to hire better, invent more significantly and connect to a broader view of the world. Sometimes, it takes time to change people's perspectives to willingly work with or for someone who doesn't look or sound like them. But when people realize that each of us is first a talented person with a colorful story and experiences, we can then develop the confidence to create one that is yet even grander and more compelling. We are no longer a melting pot; we are a mixed salad. We have our unique attributes that add great value when united. E Pluribus Unum – out of many, one – it works in a country and it works in a company.

Fix your office surroundings or 4 white walls get me out of here!

Although we may all dream of having a cool funky space for work such as the likes of the Google® offices, for most existing companies quick fixes to the current office surroundings can help inspire creativity in the workplace. Research suggests that white walls are the death of creativity. Studies indicate that painting walls in blue or green can inspire creativity. Adding some plants and some inspiring posters can change the office atmosphere quickly and inexpensively. Why not give it a try today?

Stop the 'Busyness' to get on with the Business of Innovation

One of the things that used to make me want to tear my hair out as a senior manager was the culture of 'Busyness' that surrounded me. Everyone was so 'busy' all the time (not too busy to check their social networks though). Most disturbingly our managers would walk around in a cloud of 'Busyness'. You would often hear sighs and moans emanating from their mouths. From where I stood all I could see was that those who were always 'Busy' achieved far less than others who just got on with the job at hand. 'Busyness' seemed to go hand in hand with people wanting to look important and powerful. Often this 'Busyness' was accompanied by walking around with bits of paper in hand. Not sure what that's all about but seemed like a complete waste of trees to me!

The 'Busyness' was contagious too, it seemed everyone wanted a slice of the action. Indeed, there were long days where not much more than 'Busyness' was actually going on. Trying to create an innovative business, to disrupt well-entrenched business models, amongst all of this 'busyness' was frustrating to say the very least. The 'Busyness' did however; make innovation a far more difficult task than it should have been.

The notion of 'Busyness' creates a workplace where innovation is stifled. It creates closed minds. It stifles creativity. It makes change the enemy. It means long days without getting much achieved. But help is at hand.

There's an old saying that goes

"If the first thing you do when you wake up in the morning is eat a live frog, then nothing worse can happen for the rest of the day!"

The world renowned and best-selling author and management coach, Brian Tracy wrote a great book based on this, titled 'Eat That Frog'[1]. Brian's book provides a fantastic method for your managers and staff to stop procrastinating and manage their time while having a bit of fun in the process. In his book Brian Tracy says that your "frog" is the most important thing you must do in your ~~day. You must eat your~~ "frog" first thing.

[1] Eat that Frog!: 21 great ways to stop procrastinating and get more done in less time 2nd Edition, Berrett-Koehler Publishers 2007

Great advice not only to the procrastinators, but also a wonderful way to stop the "Busyness" in your business.

Over the years in a number of situations I have had my managers, team leaders and staff read Brian's book with some great results. Once read, when someone answered the question "how are you?" with "I'm so busy", I could tell him or her to "go eat frogs". You have no idea how satisfying that can be!

To create a culture where innovation can flourish in your business - get rid of the 'Busyness' and get on with business with a new diet of frogs. Bon appetite!!

What's Next?

In this chapter we've looked at creating workplaces that are innovation incubators with flexible and adaptive work practices and environments that enhance creativity. We've also looked at how Diversity helps us create a space for innovation. We've looked at the new trend that is the disruption of business models and we've learned something to add to our daily menu. Now that you have a workplace that is conducive to innovation we need to look at how we create innovative new products and services.

Over to you!

Time to think about your own business again. Spend some time now jotting down your thoughts and answering the questions below.

Are my employees actively engaged in creative idea generation?	
Is there too much "busyness" going on in my business?	
How Diverse is my workplace?	
What are some ways I could involve my customers in creating new products/services?	

3 CRACKING THE DISRUPTION CODE

"We cannot solve a problem by using the same kind of thinking we used when we created them".

Albert Einstein

Design Thinking Means Business.

Designers have been doing it to create innovation forever; business is finally catching on. So what is it? Design Thinking of course! But what is Design Thinking?

When I was first introduced to the paradigm of Design Thinking, I remember thinking to myself, this isn't new to me. In fact I had been using Design Thinking throughout my own career – I just now had a label for it.

So you might be saying but what is Design Thinking? When we think of Design we most often think of an object. However, the word design becomes a powerful tool when we use it as a verb. Design Thinking provides the mindset and the tools to empower us to discover, define and solve problems. Design Thinking is an iterative approach that enables us to find human needs and turn them into products and services that people will buy. Using Design Thinking as a process helps us to discover opportunities and solve problems.

Design Thinking uses customer-centricity, collaboration, empathy and intuition in its problem solving methodology that starts with finding and defining problems. Design

Thinking creates multiple solutions that are tested. It helps us create hypotheses to test resulting in real data for analysis.

Wikipedia® [2]describes it as the *"design-specific cognitive activities that designers apply during the process of designing"*. I think of it as the 'Scientific Method' or 'Engineering Method' of Design for business.

Design Thinking is a holistic way of thinking that combines elements of possibility with hypothesis testing. At its essence are the following:

- Optimism
- Ideation
- Abductive Thinking
- Open Mindedness
- Creative Thinking
- Systems Thinking
- Customer Co-creation
- Comfort with Ambiguity
- Empathy and Human Centeredness
- Collaboration
- Visualization
- Iteration

---

[2] Wikipedia

Now you are probably thinking what on earth has empathy and intuition got to do with business? Isn't business about rationality and coming up with one solution to a problem quickly? This is the traditional notion of business, i.e. we aren't getting enough business we have a problem. We need empathy in our design, because the problems we are solving are not our own, they are our customers or potential customers problems.

David Kelley from IDEO describes Design Thinking as, *"It is a radical notion, in its way: the idea that creativity can be summoned at will, with a process not unlike the scientific method. That contradicts what most people have always thought. That to be creative, an angel of the Lord appears and tells you what to do."* Radical notion or not when implemented into business, Design Thinking works to create new possibilities for business.

Jeanne Liedtka from the Darden Business School, who is a wonderful proponent of Design Thinking for business, describes it as *"a process of continuously redesigning a business to achieve both product and process innovation"*. The design process can be described in a number of ways.

Research shows that there a number of different techniques and tools used in to create Design Thinking mindsets in business to promote change and innovation, but the core of the process remains the same. Design Thinking enables problems and solutions to co-evolve.

It is important to remember that Design Thinking is fundamentally about thinking like a designer. It's a mindset, a way of thinking differently about how we solve problems. As business people we like to use processes, with Design Thinking at the core of those processes, innovation and change happen. Let's look at a few examples.

"The focus on design-led innovation helped Philips Lighting® to transform itself over the past decade from a company that simply pushed products into the market into one that designs them with customer desires in mind," says CEO Rudy Provoost. Philips Lighting is no longer just about light bulbs, but providing ambience for customers. Provoost says " the company hopes to provide the bulbs and software to enable consumers to be their own lighting designers".

In Australia, Suncorp leads the way with the integration of Design Thinking into the creation new products and services. Providing it with the ability to remain highly competitive with the major banks and the ability to offer unique services to its customers.

Not only is Design Thinking useful in the creation of new products and services but also in business strategy design, business analysis, business development, and marketing and sales. In fact, when used properly, the process of Design Thinking becomes a powerful tool in building brands and growing businesses.

The Design Thinking Process that fits translates well within business and is the easiest to follow and understand is described by Jeanne Liedtka and Tim Ogilvie in their book *Designing for Growth,* through the process of What Is?, What If, What Wows?, and What Works?

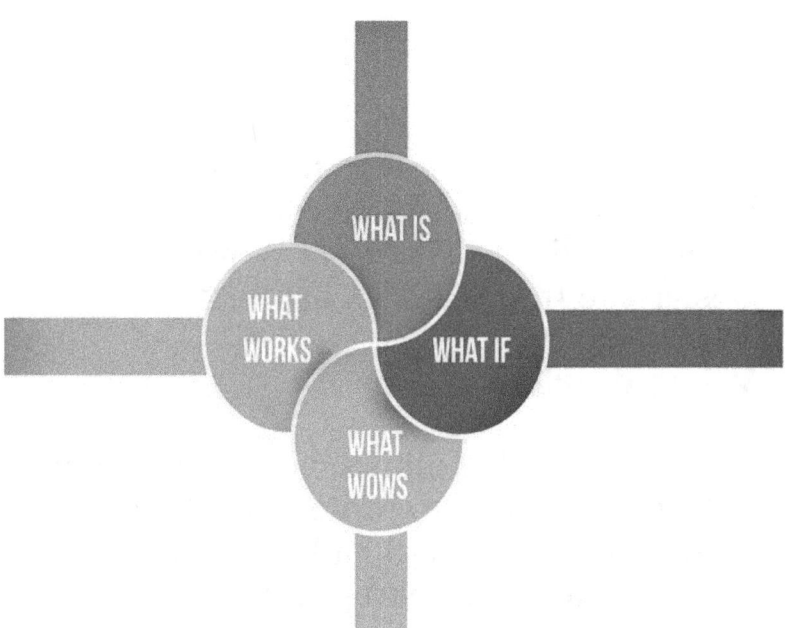

What Is?

The What Is? is the first clue in our journey to unlock the secrets of the Disruption Code. The What Is? helps us find problems and the unmet needs of our customers to create new and innovative ideas and solutions. We will return to this in a moment.

What If?

The What If? allows us to think as if there is no box and dream the impossible. This is the Divergent Thinking stage. We'll learn more about this and find some great tools to find the What If? in Chapter 4 Dreaming the Impossible and Challenging the Status Quo.

What Wows?

The What Wows helps us to focus on the best of the best ideas that can be commercialized. The What Wows? helps us Design the Impossible (Chapter 5).

What Works?

The What Works? allows us to be scientists, to test, iterate and to prototype. It also gives us permission to Fail Fast and Often and celebrates our learning experiences (Chapter 7).

I also like to add What Next?, to the process. This takes Design Thinking for business to the next level by giving us a plan for the future.

Cracking the Disruption Code.

In chapter 1 we looked at how change is affecting our entire way of life and how businesses are run today. With the imperative of innovation that exists in business within the current change paradigm, Design Thinking gives us a simple yet powerful framework to disrupt and innovate. The What Is? Is the first secret to cracking the Disruption Code.

What Is?

The first clue to cracking the disruption code relates to the What Is? of Design Thinking. Here we will look at a number of Design tools that you can use to start your own repertoire of tools to create value for your business.

The What Is? is the first clue to Disruption and Innovation for business. It is what I like to call the problem finding stage, or finding the right problem stage of the process and where customer centrism, intuition and empathy come out to play. Often we think we know what the problem is and Business leaders often jump straight into problem solving at this point. Traditional business schools actually teach us to do that. They teach us that we must use data to solve problems, but what data is relevant to our customers? Business managers that are on the back foot often have to solve or fix problems. They get caught up in the what's not working. This is often reactive not responsive behavior. Understanding our customer's emotions is a powerful tool for business. Why?, because emotions drive actions!

Microsoft recently suggested that our customer intentions are driven by four moments being 1. I want to know, 2. I want to go, 3. I want to do and 4. I want to buy. Having insight into how our customer's emotions drive their consumer behaviors helps us to solve ambiguous or ill-defined problems.

The What Is? allows us to slow down, find and define customer's unmet needs or problems. The What Is? is where you ask yourself, what problem am I solving for my customer? The What Is? stage is where we explore current realities. In this stage we look at what customers are struggling with and what frustrates them. It's also at this stage that design thinking considers an idea's potential to create value. As part of this analysis, we need to assess our own organization's capabilities and resources.

The What Is? allows us to think like a Forensic Scientist, looking for hypotheses and questions to understand our customers. During the What Is? you must continually ask the question Why? Why? Why? Just like we did when we were young. Always questioning what the problem is, remaining curious. Sounds simple but doing it right is the most important part of Cracking the

Disruption Code and the stages of Design Thinking methodology.

"One has to passionately believe it is possible to change the industry, to turn it on its head, to make sure that it will never be the same again."

Richard Branson

When we use the tools of Design Thinking's What Is? we enhance 'strategic innovation', through the discovery of what our customer's unmet or unknown needs or wants truly are.

An essential part of the What Is? in Design Thinking is the involvement of the customer in the process. Let's have a look at how customer co-creation is helping businesses to create innovative new products and services.

Customer Co-creation for Innovation

The conditions of innovation are not just about the end result; they are also about the experience. This trend is what has come to be known as co-creation – a term coined by University of Michigan professors, Venkat

Ramaswamy and C. K. Prahalad, to describe the collaborative relations between consumers and companies. Co-creation has been a trend since the 1990's when Pine and Gillmore dubbed it the "experience economy". Co-creation is the practice of allowing customers to "build their own" products and services, a practice that is gaining quite a traction among worldwide online retailers. Consumers are both the market and the partners in growing companies.

Co-creation is being defined by innovative consumerism at its best and enables consumers to be part of a company's growth. A vital part of business success is the ability for a company to quickly recognize the creations coming from consumers and learning from consumers the kind of product or service they desire. The ingredients of co-creation are then, first an ability to know your consumers and how they can be better served. Second, co-creation is about customer engagement and experience in the market segment being addressed, good general intelligence and the ability to communicate and receive ideas.

Customers Creating their very Own Products

There is a new wave of consumerism sweeping the planet where customers are creating their own products. This is an innovative practice that satisfies customer needs whilst engaging them in an interactive building experience through social co-creation.

The custom Messenger bag producers, Rickshaw Bagworks® enables it's customers to design their own bags. Sportswear vendor Shortomatic® offers custom designed swimwear. Many global e-commerce leaders such as NikeiD®, Dell®, Blue Nile®, for example have begun combining customer co-creation with social media tools where their customers can share what they have created across social networks.

NikeiD® was the first to offer a highly visual "build your own shoe" application on it's website. This led to an increase in online sales of 25% from approximately $208 million dollars to $260 million dollars in 2009. NikeID's® custom design app also surpassed $100 million dollars in sales.

The most recent example of true customer co-creation is again from Nike® with their latest shoe the 'Fly ease'. This shoe basically unpeels to take on and off and was created hand in hand with a customer with cerebral palsy. The customer who was just about to move out of home for the first time was worried about how he was going to tie his shoes on his own. He wrote to Nike® about his problem and Nike®, worked hand in hand with the customer to create this wonderful innovation in sport shoes. This is truly customer co-creation at its finest. Nike® , together with their customer solved a problem, that will help many people with disabilities into the future.

There are some great examples of customer co-creation marketplaces like Zazzle®, CafePress® and SpreadShirt® that allow consumers to design and sell their own creations. These sites have built-in design tools and e-commerce functionality. According to Zazzle® by using this business model, it has grown it's site traffic by 1600% and its sales by 900% and reports 20 million unique site visitors per month using the customer co-creation model. I am sure most businesses would envy that!

CafePress® (the popular t-shirt and gift site) claims that it has 1.1 million unique visitors to its website per month and approximately 2000 independent shops added each day. Through customer co-creation it now has 250 million unique products listed on its site.

Blue Nile®, a leader in the popular "build-your-own-ring" application indicates that since introducing customer co-creation into its business model its net sales have increased by 18.7% to $74.1 million. This was the highest first quarter sales levels in the company's history. Other custom ring sites include Brilliant Earth® and Gemvara®.

Papa John's® Facebook® page has over 1.1 million "likes" and Facebook® users are able to select pizza toppings to create a customer pizza. Another example is the Lego® Factory, where kids design new Lego® models using a digital designer app and can also submit their creations to compete.

Microsoft® supports over 1,200 of its employees participating the blogosphere to actively engage in dialogue with customers. In doing so, Microsoft® too has begun to co-create.

The iPod/Tunes/Life are the brainchild of an organization that extends the credo of its founder, Steve Jobs. However, the real genius of Steve Jobs lies in being able to "really stitch" technology with human interaction at a level that isn't duplicated elsewhere in the advanced consumer electronics marketplace.

There are now also a growing number of startups that are capitalizing on the co-creation trend on specific verticals like dress shirts (Blank-Label®, ShirtsMyWay®, ProperCloth®), chocolate bars (Chocri®, Chocomize®), jewelry (Gemkitty®, Delusha®, Art of Jewels®) and cereal (MixMyGranola, MeandGoji) that reinforce the theory that customers are increasingly demanding the ability to create their own products. (There is also a growing trend in companies that don't put spaces between words in their names. Is this Disruption in business naming?).

Customer Co-creation as Open Innovation

Customer co-creation is at its heart a form of Open Innovation. Fundamentally it's where a company can succeed in both incremental and disruptive innovation without the need to recruit people for research.

Traditional research and development diminishes the concept of open innovation. Co-creation works best when build on a strong community of diverse consumers. The essence is for people to share ideas, build on each other's work, critique, praise and compete – to become an elite brand. The real art is synthesizing all ideas and understanding the big, unlooked for themes that underpin the concept of Open Innovation.

There are no silly ideas in Open Innovation. All ideas are attempt to solve an intelligently defined problem. Companies are starting to embrace Open Innovation as part of their overall Innovation strategies.

Crowdsourcing Ideas

Social media and the crowdsourcing of ideas for co-creation is beginning to play a significant role in fuelling growth in business. Our customers are telling us what they want or don't want for that matter through the variety of social media platforms. The new commons created through social media enhances our ability for new insights into our customer's lives.

Co-creation becomes Open Innovation with the "wisdom of the crowds". (Kind of like democracy is supposed to work), "bringing the outside in", and has turned the notion of market research into a far more dynamic and creative process.

Companies that recognize consumers as a source for creativity are guaranteed to be successful in the long term. It is the customers that make corporate existence possible. Co-creation and Open Innovation thus makes it possible for companies to listen to consumers and to ensure that products and services maintain relevance in today's rapidly changing world.

Reframing the Question

So how do we begin to think differently when asking the What Is? question? Mastering the ability to reframe questions is a valuable tool in creating innovation. It's actually easier than you think, for example if asked the question – What is 50 + 50? The answer of course is 100. Asking the question in this way gives us only one answer. By reframing the question to ask, What 2 numbers add up to 100? gives us a multitude of answers. Reframing the question is the core of the What Is?

When we are thinking about the What Is? to design a new service or product we can use reframing the question to come up with great new ideas. Reframing the question helps us to look at things from other perspectives. Albert Einstein is quoted as saying that

"A problem can never be solved from the context in which it arose".

Reframing the question helps us to look at things from a completely different angle.

Just think about it. If you are out with friends on the weekend you might ask yourself the question, what movies could we see for fun tonight? This will give you a list of possible movies to go see. If you reframe the question to ask what can we do for fun tonight?, this opens up a wide range of possibilities depending on your interpretation of fun.

Another example might be, if you wanted to design a dining room table, you might ask questions like what will it be made of?, how long will it be? To create innovation you would reframe the question to ask, how do people like to experience dining? Now, the answer to this question could now result in something very different from the conventional dining table. Exciting isn't it!!

The Tools for What Is?

You might now be asking how can I come up with my own What Is? There are some wonderful tools around that will help you with finding your What Is? Some of them you will recognize. Many involve customer co-creation. Here are just a few:

Mind Mapping

Perhaps one of the most recognizable of all the tools of the What Is? is the Mind Map. It provides a visual of our ideas and shows the interactions between ideas. A mind map is a diagram that visually organizes information. Ideas are represented as images and words branching out from a central concept. They are a great way of contextualizing ideas.

There are some great mind mapping software tools available to you, if you want to show your mind maps to others. Examples include: Mindjet, XMind, Coggle, Freemind and Mindnode.

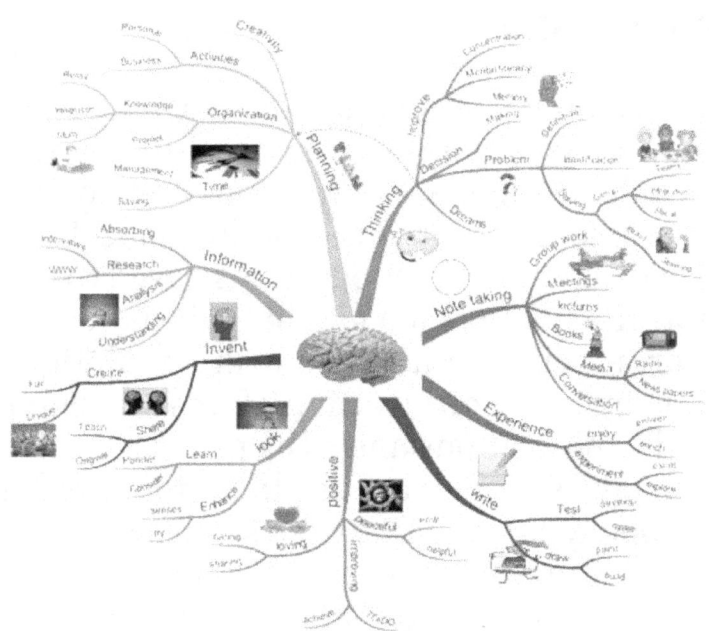

Mind Mapping – Creative Brain Example

Immersion

Immersion is a powerful tool in the What is? of Design Thinking. Immersion is the complete involvement in an activity or interest. By immersing yourself in with your customers you learn more about their experience. Immersion gives you a glimpse into people's feelings and interactions. Immersion is also where we get our inspiration. There is no better way to gain understanding of others than by immersing yourself in people's lives or communities.

Ethnography

Ethnography is a qualitative research methodology that provides us with empirical data on customers and societies and don't businesses just love data and lots of it! In Design Thinking ethnography is used to capture human behaviors in their natural environment. Creative innovative solutions come from the observation of unarticulated needs, motivations and drivers. Ethnography gives us insights into attitudes and behaviors and finds the stories that explain the why. The ethnography for business can include:

- Observation,
- Situational Analysis,

- Interviewing,
- Participant Observation.

Customer Journey Mapping

A customer journey map (sometimes called a touch point map) is essentially a visual or graphic interpretation of the journey of the customer and the touch points with a product or service. It is a visual representation of the various touch points in their interaction with a brand, product or service over time and across channels. A customer journey map is the overall story from the individual's perspective andemphasizes customer expectations and business requirements.

Placing yourself in the customer's shoes and indeed gaining feedback from your customers about their journey is a great way to ensure their needs are met in the development of products and services.

Role Playing

Sometimes referred to as body storming, role-playing is the practice of pretending or taking on the persona of the customer to experience what they do in different spaces and situations. Role-playing in business is like experimenting with an experience. Just a word of warning, the introverts in the room may not want to play this game but they can be put to good use as observers.

Mood Boards

A mood board is a visual collage that provides a representation of what a customer is looking for. Mood boards are a great way to visualize current and future realities and for getting your creative juices flowing. Mood Boards are great for gathering ideas and inspiration before you start brainstorming. You can create mood board on your computer, but its just as easy and a great way to get the 'feel' of something if you use words and pictures cut from magazines.

Mood Boards bring creativity to business.

Sounds like fun? It's not only great fun these are great methods for bringing out the creative brain in business people. When combined with modern and traditional business methodologies, Design Thinking becomes a simple yet powerful tool in our everyday business.

Big Data and its use in Social Mapping – taking Design one step further.

With the advent of the Digital Era, we now live in a world of countless interactions and transactions. This digital universe has now grown to over 2 trillion gigabytes. Every time we use the Internet we leave a shadow of our interactions. These interactions create what is called Big Data.

Facebook®, Google®, Twitter®, Amazon® and many others use this Big Data as a way of mapping consumers online spending and other habits. From this information they can create social maps of our behaviour including things like, what gender we are, how old we are, where we live (right down to our house and street number), what we like to buy, when we like to buy it and how we share information on the products we have bought across social media platforms. Just think about that when next you share what you have bought on Facebook® and Twitter®.

Although you may not have access to the levels of Big Data that Facebook® and the likes have, if you have a good CRM platform in place you can keep similar data on your customers and use it to create a Social Map of their behaviours to determine their needs. A very useful tool for the What Is?

The What Is? for Everyday Business

The What Is? is a powerful tool in our

everyday business. You can use it for a variety of things. For example it's a great tool to look at current realities, analyzing our businesses, preparing for innovation in tendering, planning for marketing and creating new services and products and much more. It gives us the competitive advantage by enabling a customer centric focus.

The What is? can be used to find the "Us" and "Them". More than a traditional SWOT analysis, the What is? allows us to think much more creatively about our business and our competitors with the customer experience in mind. It helps to create very different value propositions. The What is? gives business the ability to remain agile and responsive by enhancing our ability to engage and co-create with our customers.

The What Is? and Business Model Disruption

The What Is? helps to disrupt current business models. Recall the great examples of Business Model Disruption like Amazon® and Apple®. Amazon® is the largest bookseller in the world and achieved this through Business Model Disruption. The businesses of the now and of the future have created entirely new business models. Now think about Uber® and Airbnb®. These two businesses run on what is now called the 'sharing or peer- to-peer economy'. The success of Uber® and Airbnb® comes from their disruptive business models that use the peer-to-peer or sharing economy. Both companies have disrupted their spaces by attacking an existing market that was traditionally dominated by entrenched companies that were inefficient or expensive. For example, Uber® recognized the customer need for quick easy and inexpensive transportation services. Traditional taxi companies are a great example of this. Most of us can relate to poor service, dirty and smelly taxis (surprisingly not in France where the taxis are the cleanest I have ever seen), and high costs. Strict controls and regulations in the taxi industry have given rise to limited competition and 'fat and lazy' taxi companies (usually monopolies or duopolies), ripe for disruption. AirBnb's® business model uses a world wide network of people who will happily share their space with others. This is now a multi-billion dollar business providing accommodation across the world. AirBnb does this without owning a single hotel anywhere.

Is your industry at risk of loosing business to a smart start up like Uber® or AirBnb®?

Through the lens of the What Is? we can look at what is happening in our own industry, in other industries and review our value chain and customer touch points. Customer Journey Mapping and Co-creation provide us with excellent tools to unlock new innovations and opportunities for innovating our business model. Just thinking about the customer experience and their fears and wants, helps us in the development of a new product or service.

What's Next?

In this chapter we've looked at the What Is? and some great tools you can use to seek out problems that your customer's or indeed the world needs solutions to. You now have a few clues to cracking the innovation mystery and have commenced gathering your own repertoire of tools that you can use in your day-to-day practice. We've also looked at Customer Co-Creation and Disruption of Business Models. Now that you've looked at the What Is? and possibly started to come up with some great problems that meet your customer's unmet needs what's next? - Using the What If? to dream the impossible and challenge the status quo!

Over to you!

The What Is? for Your Business

Now it's your turn! Can you think of some creative ways to use the What Is? in your business? What Is? your current business model? What Is? the business model used by your competitors? How will you use customer co-creation to help your business innovate? Take some time to jot down your ideas and visualize them. Maybe create a Mood Board that represents your current industry?

What is my current business model?	
What are my competitors doing differently?	
What are other industries doing differently?	

What Design Thinking tools can I implement into my business practice today?	

4 DREAMING THE IMPOSSIBLE AND CHALLENGING THE STATUS QUO

"Here's to the crazy ones. The misfits. The rebels. The troublemakers. The round pegs in the square holes. The ones who see things differently. They're not fond of rules. And they have no respect for the status quo. You can quote them, disagree with them, glorify or vilify them. About the only thing you can't do is ignore them. Because they change things. They push the human race forward. And while some may see them as the crazy ones, we see genius. Because the people who are crazy enough to think they can change the world, are the ones who do."

Apple Inc.

New Ideas for Innovation

In chapter 3 we looked at the What Is? in Design Thinking for Business. The next clue to cracking the Disruption Code is the Design Thinking stage that is the What If? This is where you can let yourself go! Become one of the 'crazy ones... the misfits and the troublemakers' and allow yourself to think not only outside the box but as if there was no box. At the What If? stage we are not looking for the 'right' idea we are looking for lots of ideas. The more the merrier. We want ideas that challenge the ordinary or the status quo. The What If? is all about ideation where you use both your conscious and subconscious mind for imagination. It is highly important that judgment is left at the door.

Divergent Thinking

During the What If? we are looking for 'Divergent Thinking'. So what is divergent thinking? Psychologist J.P. Guilford first invented the terms convergent thinking and divergent thinking back in 1967. Divergent thinking is the spontaneous non-linear flow of multiple ideas on a given topic. Divergent thinking is the basis of our creativity. It is what is responsible for the 'aha' moments we often have in the shower in the morning.

Change Management During the What If?

The What If? stage is the time when you may get some kickback from your team. It's where the challenges of change management come back into play. During the What If? the doubters can come out to play if we allow them to. People often start to bring in their biases, judgments and objections. Managers often revert to managing risk and problem solving. Factors that can halt the process of Design Thinking such as playing the Devil's advocate, fear and resistance introduce destructive negativity and need to be put in their place. During the What If? process, managers must leave any notion of risk fly for the time being. Leave the 'Black Hat' outside, ask the naysayers to leave and tie down the problem solvers at this point. You and your team must bring what the Zen Buddhists call the 'beginner's mind". In other words, fresh and new ideas, an attitude of openness, eagerness and a lack of preconceptions, just like when you are beginning to learn brand new things.

The What if? is the ideas stage where it is imagination not problem solving we need. How do you counter objections in the What If? – counter objections with a reframed question or by asking the question "but what if it worked?" Try this out next time you get an objection to one of your ideas.

So how do we put the What If? into practice?

Brainstorming

"Think left and think right and think low and think high. Oh, the thinks you can think up if only you try!"

Theodore Lesieg (Dr. Suess)

Traditionally when we think of brainstorming we picture groups of people sitting together in a room shouting out new ideas to a facilitator at the front of the room. Brainstorming in this sense is most often used in the problem-solving sphere. In the What If? of Design Thinking we are not looking for the answers or solutions at this stage of the process. Instead we are looking for a large quantity of ideas. We are not looking or judging ideas for quality. We just want ideas to flow.

Set aside your traditional notions of Brainstorming. Brainstorming in the Design Thinking process is best done by individuals outside of the group process. We put group brainstorming and the notion of building on and extending others ideas aside during the Brainstorming in Design Thinking. Individual brainstorming can generate far more ideas than the traditional methods because there is no fear of being judged.

Serviette Brainstorming

Have you ever been in a coffee shop and seen people jotting down notes on their Serviette or Coaster? It seems we get a lot of great ideas sitting drinking our favorite beverage. Perhaps coffee makes us open our minds to new ideas or it's just that we have time to think in these places. Whatever it is Serviette Brainstorming is a great way for you to come up with new ideas during the What If? of Design

Thinking. Of course you may wish to take a few serviettes of your own to the local coffee shop so that you've got lots of room to draw and jot down your ideas. Oh and please don't write them on the coffee shop or restaurant's linen serviettes or you will definitely not be welcomed back. Sit back enjoy your coffee, tea, or dare I say a wine and let those creative ideas flow! (No cloth serviettes were harmed in the writing of this book).

Grab a coffee and some serviettes and away you go!

Lots and lots of Sticky Notes

Have you ever had a brilliant idea either just before bed or in the middle of having some fun and you think to yourself *'that's a great idea I'll have to remember that!.'* Then you rack your brains for days trying to remember that moment of pure brilliance. Okay, that's the reason sticky notes were invented. Keep a stack of them, oh and a pen of course, on your bedside table and when you have that moment, write down your idea.

Of course in today's digital world we also have access to digital forms of sticky notes on our phones. If you wish you can use an app like Evernote or OneNote to make sure you don't forget your moments of brilliance.

During the What If?, try bringing together your sticky notes with those of others and stick them up on a wall or board. This brings a wealth of brilliant moments together in one place.

Metaphors

In business we have all heard the metaphor 'time is money'. Now we all know that time and money are really two different things, but this is a great way of solving the 'get on with the business of business' problem. Well if 'time is money" metaphors are the "silver bullet" to creative thinking. Metaphors are commonly used to help solve complex problems. ("Eat that Frog" is a Metaphor) In Design Thinking we use metaphors to juxtapose unfamiliar problems onto familiar situations to make them easier to understand.

The What If? and Collaboration

During the What If? we want to think big. We want to think about what may seem the impossible. To create innovation, during the What If? we are looking for those big gnarly problems that need solving and diverse thinking in order to pre-empt markets. This is a tall order if left to one team or internal innovation hub. How do we ensure we have a range of possibilities to test?

This is where collaboration with others comes in to play. Through collaboration, we find new and wonderful ideas we may not have thought about previously.

The Importance of Internal Collaboration for Innovation

Innovation embraces the ability to pre-empt markets; foster, protect and license ideas and know-how; source funding and execute a timely, profitable commercialization strategy.

Collaborative innovation is successful when it bridges the gap between flexible organizational structure and a quality driven workforce whose imaginative capability is freed but focused. The synergy is achieved through a top-down drive that encourages participation and stimulates creativity, with ideas being created, nurtured and harvested.

Reaching this performance nirvana usually needs more than just an organizational overhaul. It needs to be buried into the DNA of management. Continuous Quality Improvement and Continuous Innovation should be the focus of action, with the entire organization configured for both quality and innovation, but this alone is not enough.

As we know, we live in a highly networked world with a growing knowledge-based economy; counterproductive to this is people working in silos, either unaware of, or unwilling to share knowledge and ideas. For decades now, researchers as well as industrialists have echoed the sentiment that collaboration would change the very DNA of corporate culture and management within a company thereby impacting on both profitability and sustainability. The collaboration of a cross-functional team (for example; marketing, sales, product development, finance and Human Resources) can potentially open up multiple new ventures and initiatives.

Collaboration provides us with a decentralized, participatory approach to innovation, based on the premise that innovation is more effective when multiple partners are working together. Open innovation, when used as internal collaboration reduces costs and shortens time to market and opening up of new streams of revenue.

Internal collaboration for innovation creates a two-way knowledge exchange that includes both an inflow and outflow of knowledge. It can be the perfect solution to supplement a constrained internal Research and Development department that is slowing down product development. For it to work effectively however, certain cultural elements have to be in place for a dependable internal collaboration structure to be built upon including empowering people to make decisions.

A report from the Organisation for Economic Co-operation and Development OECD[3] (2013) clearly showed the correlation between internal collaborations in a company to its partnerships and willingness to work with numerous external partners. It isn't enough having knowledge freely available in the market. A firm needs both the resources and the capabilities to use this knowledge. These resources and capabilities can be built through internal collaboration.

There are several tangible benefits to internal collaboration. These include knowledge sharing, risk mitigation, cost reduction, faster speed to product development and go to market. This however, doesn't mean that we offset or ignore any threats or possible disadvantages of internal collaboration – the blatantly visible – harmonizing

---

[3] OECD (2013), *OECD Science, Technology and Industry Scoreboard 2013: Innovation for Growth*, OECD Publishing, Paris.

different viewpoints and ideas collected. This is where Design Thinking can help us.

Internal collaboration isn't only about increasing productivity inside the organization; it also enables the mechanisms to cope with external collaborations. In fact the need of internal collaboration is the drive behind the current $4.77B to the estimated $8.19B market of Enterprise Social Software and Internal Collaborations platforms (ReportsnReports.com). The fundamental reason for such an explosive growth and central theme is the ability to offer a systems approach that incorporates people, processes and technology to any given problem. It does however, need the mindset that *'the whole is greater than the sum of its parts"* (Aristotle).

We are quickly moving to a world where internal collaboration is innovating itself. In fact, the world is looking for platforms and solutions that can deliver a marketplace of ideas and execute them.

External Partners and Collaboration

With disruption abound, companies are now partnering to collaborate on new and exciting products and long-term sustainability. Indeed in the current climate, many companies do not have the internal resources to go it alone. The possibilities are abound from these partnerships. Additionally, many companies now partner with universities for innovation to do away with the need for internal Research and Development departments. This gives them the competitive edge in designing new products and services by working with creative and clever people.

The speed of change in technology provides us with an imperative for external collaboration. Collaboration and co-competition with others is now becoming a critical ingredient for businesses to keep pace. In fact external collaboration has become critical for speed to market. It might seem counterintuitive to competitiveness to collaborate with others in your industry; however, companies that are doing this are growing together.

Through external collaboration, businesses are joining their creativity, resources and creating new economies of scale, in the development of new products and services. By looking for external partnerships companies are innovating much faster than ever before. Just imagine the What If? that could be created with external collaboration!

Partnerships for collaboration across industries provide the opportunity to strengthen both partners' capabilities. Can you think of external collaborative partners that may be suitable for your business to work with?

Collaborative Software Solutions

As we have seen many of the brightest ideas for innovation come from internal and external collaboration. Yet few organizations have the systems in place to make collaboration happen. Collaborating for innovation often takes second place to the day-to-day running of a business and ideas often get lost on spreadsheets (how I loath spreadsheets). Other issues that affect our ability to collaborate are the nature of silos created by divisions and geographical spread.

In order to foster innovation in your business you must develop places for ideas to come together and where people can work together creatively, come up with ideas and problem solve. This is where software becomes our savior!

Using a great collaboration software platform can help foster innovation makes collaboration and ideation fun and easy, saves money and time and brings divisions and geographically diverse teams together. There are a number of collaboration tools on the market that will foster innovation mindsets in your business. My favorite is a program called Crowdicity®, which is based on the concepts of Design and uses social sharing and gamification to make idea generation fun. Why not check out a few for your organization. Just think how you could make your business grow!

What's Next?

In this chapter we have used divergent thinking and explored a number of tools and ideas to help us unlock the Disruption Code to enable us to find some wonderful What Ifs? By now you should have a wealth of ideas that may or may not be commercially viable. The next key to cracking the Disruption Code and unlocking innovation in your business and finding the best of these ideas is the What Wows?

Over to you!

Think about the ways you have traditionally conducted ideas generation sessions in your business. Spend some time answering the following questions.

How can I integrate the What if? into our next strategy session?	
How will I change the traditional brainstorming mentality in my business?	
Who will buy the Serviettes?	
What software would help our company to collaborate?'	

5 UNLOCKING THE WOW

*"Design is not just what it looks like and feels like.
Design is how it works."*

Steve Jobs

Now you have so many great ideas what are you going to do with them? The next clue in the Disruption Code is where we unlock the What Wows?

What Wows?

In the What Wow's stage of the Design Thinking process for business we revisit the wealth of ideas generated in the What If? stage of our journey. At this point we need to now look for a manageable number of ideas and the ideas that really 'pop'. The 'Wow' ideas are the ones that provide optimum balance between solving a problem for the customer whilst also offering an attractive profit proposition. The What Wows? is an iterative process where we test our assumptions and work through our ideas and look at potential outcomes.

In the What Wow's we develop rapid prototypes of our products or services and test/retest them. The What Wow's is where 'Convergent Thinking' comes into play. The What Wows? is also where we use 99% perspiration instead of inspiration. It is the hypothesis testing stage in the Scientific Method where we experiment with our ideas through iteration.

Convergent Thinking for the What Wows?

The notion of Convergent Thinking as coined by Joy Paul Guilford is the opposite of Divergent Thinking and it means coming up with a single well-established answer to a problem. This is where the traditional analytic manager's brain takes over.

You might be saying finally! Yes now it is time to allow your analytical brain to come out. The What Wows?, is the phase of Design Thinking where you can now start to analyse and make choices. According to Tim Brown, this is when "ideas come together and take form".

What is "Iteration"?

Wikipedia [4]describes "iteration" as "the act of repeating a process with the aim of approaching a desired goal, target or result. Each repetition of the process is also called an "iteration", and the results of one iteration are used, as the starting point for the next iteration. The iteration process is test, improve, retest, improve and is an important part of the development and testing of our ideas.

Data to Inform our Assumptions

In business, we rely on data for a great variety of thing however, most importantly we rely on data to inform our assumptions. In today's business world, one of the biggest challenges we face is finding data that provides us with a deep understanding of what our customers want. Often when we are bringing a brand-new product or service to market we do not have a history of data to base our assumptions on.

---

[4] Wikipedia

Our existing data sources most often give us the understanding of where our customers have been and what they might have done without an understanding of why they did what they did.

Sure we can make our assumptions based on similar projects but are these assumptions then no more than just guesses?

Throughout the What Wows? we are testing our hypothesis. During this phase we gather a significant amount of data from the feedback we receive and the prototype testing we have completed. Through the data we collect we now have valuable insights into the commercial viability of our products and a deeper understanding of how our customers interact with our product or service. Our assumptions are now more than just guesses. They are tested assumptions that allow us to more accurately forecast the costs and profitability of our ideas.

Let's take a look at some of the tools we use for iteration in the What Wows?

Rapid Prototyping and the What Wows?

Rapid prototyping for Design Thinking is the process of creating early models for products or services with end user input. This often flies in the face of conventional business wisdom where we usually don't release a product or service to our customers until it is 95% complete. This traditional process has a much higher level of cost and hence risk involved. Many hours and much money has been wasted on making a product as close to perfect as possible then releasing it to customers who, not only don't want it but ultimately won't buy it.

Design Thinking allows us to employ small-scale prototypes quickly. By doing so if changes to the design of our product or service are needed, this can be done quickly and cost effectively.

Software developers often use rapid prototyping during the beta or open sourcing stages of their product development. Creating prototypes and testing and retesting them can solve early problems. You will be surprised but your customers love to be involved in the process. Rapid prototyping helps us to fail early, re-develop quickly and find the What Wows? more efficiently.

Storytelling

Storytelling is not only a great way for you to think of new ideas and possibilities. Stories help you encourage self-reflection and can help to increase empathy. It puts people and their experience front and center. With Design Thinking you can imagine designs that improve customers lives through story telling. By being able to imagine the future of the customer and their new journey with your product and service helps with innovation.

Storytelling can be used throughout all of the stages

of Design Thinking methodology, in the What Wows? part of the process it helps you to imagine the future where people are interacting with your design. It helps you to focus in on what will work and reframe the question to see if it Wows. Storytelling also helps you clarify your ideas to prepare you for your pitch.

Great Storytelling takes the listener on a journey. To do this a great story needs not only a beginning, middle and an end, it also requires you to know your audience, present a sequence of events and the posing of questions of your audience. Now you have a story, it's time to put it into a pitch.

Pitching your ideas

Creating a great pitch for your idea is vital to its success when presenting it to the CEO or a Board. Let's face it; you are not going to be able to get the funding for your Wow ideas without support from the people that hold the purse strings.

So what do we need to do to create the perfect pitch?

Throughout the Design Thinking process you have just been through you will have great insight into the following:

- Your competition
- Your target market
- The customer need

- Your product or service's key benefits
- Your product or service's unique value propositions

However, your work is not yet done. You now need a great pitch to get your message across. The key to a perfect pitch is to keep it simple. Similar to thinking about the end users in Design Thinking you need to be thinking about the audience of your pitch. Think of it in the same way as you would an elevator pitch. Here's what you need:

- A great "hook"

Get your audience's attention with a statement or question that sparks their interest. Here is one example of a great hook for your pitch: Imagine if the next time you lost your keys there was an easy way to find them?

- A body

Create your pitch with a beginning, middle and an end. Don't go into lengthy detail. Have a more detailed report ready to give to your audience at the end.

- Show some passion and excitement

If you aren't passionate about your idea how on earth will anyone else be? Decision makers and investors expect energy and dedication.

- A request

Don't forget to ask for something at the end of your pitch. What is it you are wanting from your audience?

And whatever you do please no 'death by PowerPoint'. Many a great leader has been lost to a boring and unnecessary PowerPoint presentation!

Shelving your Not So Wow ideas

So what happens to all of those wonderful ideas that we came up with in the What If? that don't quite hit the sweet spot of What Wows? Don't throw them out just shelve them for the time being. Lots of great ideas may not pack a punch right at this moment. This can be due to timeliness of the idea. The world may not yet be ready for it. So we don't throw these ideas out we just put them somewhere safe to be revisited at a later date.

What's Next?

By now you will have come up with some amazing wow ideas that give real bang and have tested them through the rapid prototyping. You are ready to pitch your ideas to the people that hold the purse strings. Not only this you have prepared for take-off. The next stage of cracking the Disruption Code.

Over to you!

By now you have some great Wow ideas for your own business. Spend some time answering the following questions and reflecting on the Design Thinking process so far.

What are your "WOW" ideas?	
What ideas have you shelved?	
Have you got buy in for your "WOWS"?	
Which of your "WOWS" packs the greatest punch for solving your customer's problems?	

6 PREPARING FOR TAKE OFF – WHAT WORKS?

"Creativity is not the finding of a thing, but the making something out of it after it is found."

James Russell Lowell

What Works?

In chapter 5 we looked at the What Wows? The next piece of the puzzle in the Disruption Code is the What Works? of Design Thinking. The What Works? takes what we have learned from the wonderful 'as if there was no box' thinking we did in the What If? and the results of our Rapid Prototyping in the What Wows? stage coupled with our learning's from the building and testing of prototypes to a Learning Launch. Once again the customer is central to the process. Our customers are vital in this stage in order for us to minimize risks. (Yes now you can take start into account the risks.)

"A designer knows he has achieved perfection not when there is nothing left to add, but when there is nothing left to take away."

Antoine de Saint-Exupéry

During the What Works? we now get to take the outcomes of what we learnt during our low-fidelity prototype testing to the learning launch stage. Although we are selling a product to a customer or small group of customers in this stage we are still experimenting and testing in the What Works?

In this stage small groups of customers give us feedback on our product or service to enable us to refine our solutions and gain insight into their perceived value. Our customers can also help us design or re-design the final product during the What Works?

Customer Testing in the What Works? – The Learning Launch

During the What Works? we take our product or service back to the customers that helped us conceive our ideas for feedback and to check on its viability. Is the product/service solving the problem for your customer? What risks are they taking by purchasing your product over a similar product or one they may already be using?

This is known as the Learning Launch. Your customers may pay a reduce cost or a special price to use your product during this phase.

This is called a Learning Launch because it is just that. An early release of a not so perfect product that you can fix problems early and learn from any mistakes made. It forms a link between prototyping and commercialisation of your product or service and is an inexpensive mechanism to gain invaluable lessons and insights into your product's value propositions.

In order to make your Learning Launch effective, it must feel like a real launch to your customers and your team. Remember this is a Learning Launch and not a pilot – it must have an end date and important feedback points to gather data that can be used for its evaluation. In other words, plan your Learning Launch very carefully and make sure you collect relevant data.

During the Learning Launch you may be working with a customer base that you are not used to working with. Because of this you will need to be prepared for surprises and highly responsive. If not the only thing you will gain is bad feedback that possibly damages your brand. Remember this is the time of social media and the Twitter sphere, where bad experiences are shared across the world within minutes. Keep your customer group up to date with what is happening with your product and be fully transparent. These customers are helping you to co-create and are a wonderful source of new ideas to help improve your product if you treat them like co-creators. Bring them along on the journey and you will benefit greatly.

At the end of your Learning Launch send your customers a special gift to say thank you. Perhaps a discounted subscription to your final product or recognition as a founding member? Happy Learning!

Return on Investment (ROI) and the What Works? in Design Thinking

Finding the What Works? and engaging in rapid

prototyping testing and with the outcomes of and data collected during your Learning Launch, you able to far more accurately predict Return On Investment (ROI). You may now be asking how?

Have a think about what ROI is. In its simplest form, ROI has traditionally been a useful tool for business people to predict whether or not to invest in new products or services. But what is ROI calculated on? Assumptions. And what is an Assumption? A guess!

Although our assumptions are usually based on past experience or performance so they are often no more than educated guesses. Indeed, in the world of disruption, there may not be a past to extrapolate these guesses from. The What Works? and rapid prototyping gives us the foundation to better-informed assumptions in order to calculate ROI for our innovations.

As our customers have been involved in the process of testing and re-testing our prototypes, we have a much better idea of their perceived value and we may even know how much they would be willing to pay for the end product. This enables us to more accurately assume input costs and final prices.

What's Next?

In this chapter we have looked at the What Works? of Design Thinking. We have developed our prototypes and have been both the scientist and the designer through the testing phase. Our customers are our greatest allies and early adopters may have already purchased some products from this process. You are on your way, but here's where our traditional business mindset of risk aversion might come back to haunt us. In the next chapter we will look at how we view risk and failure and how we need to place the small bets to succeed.

Over to you!

Think about the methods you use, or don't use for that matter, to test your ideas. Have you ever involved your customers in testing? Answer the following questions for your own situation.

How could your customers help you in the What Works? phase?	
Do you currently use prototyping in your business?	
What do you now need to pitch your new product to the money people?	
Write down your learning's from this exercise.	

7 FAILING FAST AND CHEAP

"I've missed more than 9000 shots in my career. I've lost almost 300 games. 26 times, I've been trusted to take the game winning shot and missed. I've failed over and over and over again in my life. And that is why I succeed."

Michael Jordan

What makes innovative companies different?

Throughout our journey together we've looked at some great examples of innovative companies like Apple®, Uber® and Airbnb® and how they put creativity and innovation at the core of their DNA. But what is it that really makes them different? These companies have a low risk/failure tolerance.

Of course Failing Fast and Cheap or as its also known as Failing Fast and Often is not really about the failure, it's primarily about the learning experience that comes from failure. In traditional business models we would painstakingly make a product or service 95% right before releasing it to consumers. As you know this can be a long and costly process often still resulting in failure. The notion of Failing Fast and Cheap also helps us to take risk.

Risk and Failure – the key to success

How do we perceive failure?

During a commencement address, Apple® co-founder, Steve Jobs talked about how he dropped out of college because he felt he was wasting his parent's hard-earned money. He later went on to help develop Apple® Incorporated. After a 10 year run at the helm of Apple®, his own board of directors fired him. He later went on to help build Pixar®. Eventually, he went back to Apple® and engineered the company's triumphant return as a competitor in the marketplace. In short, Jobs looked back on his so-called failures and connected the dots. He decided that his successes would not have come about if not for his failures.

Unfortunately, many people have an unhealthy perception of failure. In addition to this, many businesses lack an environment of constructive failure. Rather than incorporating failure into the learning and business growth process, they tend to close the door on whatever component failed and ignore it completely. This method of not dealing with failure can end up costing companies in the long run because as companies evolve and change leadership, mistakes are often repeated. Creating a precedent of failures makes it easier to keep learning from past mistakes. According to Harvard professor, Rita McGrath, "You have paid your tuition (through lost revenue or operating costs), so you might as well get something out of it".

Professional athletes demonstrate this concept each time they compete. On average, baseball players will miss the ball more times than they will hit it. Football players who drop passes often attribute their successes in creating big plays to having a short memory. When a receiver drops a pass his only recourse is to shake it off and get back into the game knowing full well the he will be much more alert the next time round.

"Some people are lucky enough to go through life failing very little if at all", said Randy Komisar, founder and leader of several successful technology businesses in Silicon Valley. "These people may be lucky, but I don't think they're as wise".

The emergence of new trends and technologies has business leaders clamoring for innovation to promote leading-edge business practices. However, few industry executives embrace failure as a learning device from which successes are commonly achieved. In difficult economic times, prudence dictates that companies operate in cautionary mode taking fewer risks that might result in further loss of market share and financial turmoil. The concern with this mode of operation is that breakthroughs depend on a certain level of risks and failure.

"Failure builds character", as Bill Gates once said, "success is a lousy teacher. It seduces smart people into thinking they cant lose", failure builds character and teaches us how to be resourceful and persistent. Successes are far more rewarding when we can accept failure as a learning experience.

Failure for Business Success through Design Thinking

"A Ship in the Harbor is Safe, but that's not what Ships are Built for"

John A Shedd

It will come as no surprise to you that failures are a natural process in business. What differentiates businesses that are highly successful is that they have the mindset of analyzing their failures and where they are at and how they can use that experience to move forward. An example of this is Donald Trump, who went from being over 13 million dollars in debt to having a net worth of over 2.7 billion dollars.

As business leaders, when we are faced with failure, we have a number of options to take:

- We can blame others for them,
- We can pretend they never happened,
- We can accept responsibility for them,
- Or we can go back to the drawing board and reinvent, or develop a new prototype for our idea.

Blaming others will get you nowhere in business. Failure is a learning process. Pretending that failures never happened prevents us from exploring that experience and extracting the lesson from it. When we pretend that a failure never happened, we sweep it under the carpet and what happens? It comes right back out at a later time. By not choosing to deal with your failures, you are not learning from them, so your chance of repeating the same mistake will still be there and you are not moving forward. In the iteration process we learn from our failures and redesign them.

Now ask yourself the question, "How can I use this

failure positively in my business?" By asking this, you can effectively change a failure into an opportunity for business growth.

In fact when we look at failure in the context of Design Thinking failures become part of our testing processes. Failure is an acceptable part of the process of prototyping.

Some Great Failures Turned into Innovations.

To help fuel your inspiration and also show you that failures do in fact lead to great achievements, here are some historical icons that gave experienced more than their fair share of failures in their life before creating their innovation.

Thomas Edison failed approximately 10,000 times during his pursuit to invent the world's first light bulb. It was reported in a local newspaper of the time, that after 10,000 unsuccessful attempts to produce a sustainable light bulb, Edison's frustrated assistant told him to just give up on his failed invention. Edison countered by saying, "I have not failed. I've just found 10,000 ways that won't work". The following wee, the world witnessed the first working light bulb.

A 65 year old, Colonel Sanders, was living off a $100 social security check that he had just received.

Broke and alone, he could have blamed anyone and everyone for the poverty he was experiencing, but instead, he took responsibility for his situation and started selling fried chicken made from his mother's secret recipe. It took him an estimated 1000 house visits to sell his first order of chicken, but the rest is now history.

As a young cartoon artist, Walt Disney was told by every single newspaper editor that he contacted that he had no talent that they could use. While working on some cartoons in his run-down shed one night, a small mouse scurried out from the wall and danced across the garage floor. This mouse became the inspiration for Mickey Mouse.

Anthony Robbins, in his twenties, was bankrupt, overweight, and depressed. He developed ways to change his life for the better and is now one of the biggest names in the Personal Development Coaching Industry in the world.

These are just some of the great stories that make us recognize that we can all learn from failure and indeed turn it into success. Design Thinkers use failure as an opportunity to learn and innovate in their business. Failure is all about testing our hypothesis for our product or service. It's about learning quickly. For business failing quickly and inexpensively becomes an imperative. When we do this we stop wasting long periods of time and often lots of money creating products or services that wont work out in the marketplace. Indeed failure becomes something quite different when viewed through the lens of Design Thinking.

The Risks of Purchasing Innovation Through Acquisition

There's a growing trend for companies to purchase innovation through acquisition. Indeed innovation through acquisition and mergers can be a great growth catalyst and has become a vital complement to internal, organic innovation in a growing number of industries. When you think of companies that have been able to successfully acquire innovation, what examples come to mind? Disney's® purchase of Pixar® is just one that comes to mind for me. Today's tech industry also provides lots of examples.

A successful innovation acquisition requires a combination of blending new and old cultures together, trying to get the acquired company to continue doing what made them successful in the first place, but in a new context. The key is offering an acquired team a chance to make their beloved creation bigger and a lot more prominent. However, there is tendency for larger companies to avoid risky, costly projects that could result in disruptive innovation and after an acquisition the mistake they often make is to project this risk adversity on to the new team.

Most managers' first instinct is to acquire and integrate the new business into their current models. But more than this they can impose overwhelming structures, rules and an institutionalized 'slowness' on to the new team who are often not used to this. This can result in frustration and a loss of the creative space that inspired the innovation in the first instance. Ultimately it can lead to the loss of the creative brains to new ventures. In other words the 'Innovation Mindset' walks out the door leaving the slow and steady mindset wondering how on earth to innovate.

So yes innovation can be bought through acquisition but the important thing is to make sure the new team is given the creative space to continue to do what it is they are good at doing... embracing risk! Food for thought isn't it?

Placing Lots of Small Bets - Minimum Viable Product

To create an environment where risk and failure is okay we need to think about placing lots of small bets. We do this through the notion of 'minimum viable product' (MVP). So what is an MVP? When Eric Ries used the term for the first time he described it as: "A Minimum Viable Product is that version of a new product which allows a team to collect the maximum amount of validated learning about customers with the least effort." An MVP can make a return on investment and if thought through carefully will, but the notion is really about ensuring that consumers take up later versions of your product or service. MVP's are small risk bets that are sent to market for early adopters to test. Examples of MVPs include Beta versions of software products.

What's Next?

In this chapter we've looked at how our adversity to risk can hinder our efforts to innovate. We've also looked at how we can use failure to succeed. When we place lots of small bets with the notion of Minimum Viable Product we can minimize risk and create great new products. In the next chapter we look at the What's Next?

Over to you!

How does your organisation view risk and failure?
Now it's time to think once again about your own
business. Take the time to answer the following
questions for yourself.

Is my business highly Risk Adverse?	
Does my business suffer from Institutionalised "slowness"?	
Is my business open to the idea of Minimum Viable Product?	
Are my Managers good at Managing but inhibiting growth?	

8 WHAT'S NEXT? THIS IS NOT THE CONCLUSION

"Action is the foundational key to all success."

Pablo Picasso

Beginning your Journey

This is not the conclusion; it's just the beginning! Throughout our journey together we've looked at the conditions for innovation and change to give you the basis to save your business from becoming another statistic and to embed innovation into your business DNA.

With the imperative of "innovate or evaporate" and with the very recognition that existing companies require a regime of continuous innovation to remain competitive, the time is now to start this process for yourself. You now have the beginning of your repertoire of concepts and tools to unlock the Disruption Code and it's time to put what you've learnt into practice.

It's time now to turn transformational thinking into transformational doing. Without the What's Next? your business will become business as usual and as you have seen business as usual can no longer work in today's business world. In this Chapter we will combine some traditional ideas and tools with some new and modern business practices.

Design and Lean Startup methodology - a marriage made in heaven

Lean start up methodology as proposed by Eric Ries, has become a successful template for not only entrepreneurs but has also created many successful, intrapreneurs in the process. By coupling the notions of Lean such as the Minimum Viable Product, with Design Thinking and traditional business strategies we create a new level of business success that creates resilience, responsiveness, flexibility and adaptability for companies of any size. The combination creates the foundations for highly robust feedback systems, and more importantly provides the link into our established systems and processes. Our traditional processes create accountability for our design. Lean startup methods provide the transition between the design and traditional business processes and the opportunity for further iteration. The outcomes create a feedback loop back to design.

When all the forces are combined, they create a whole new paradigm for business success.

Developing your Business' Innovation Strategy

An Innovation Strategy defines the role, and sets the expectations for Innovation in your business. Your Innovation Strategy needs to be inspiring and set the tone for future growth and development of your business. A highly successful Innovation Strategy will set the scene for both incremental and breakthrough innovation to disrupt your industry. It's also the key to business model disruption.

In order to achieve 'buy in' from all of the key

stakeholders in your business, involve everyone in the process of its development. Your Innovation Strategy should also look at the wider world outside of your business. Your business does not exist in isolation! Most importantly, just like your business you need to make your strategy, flexible, adaptable and responsive to change. Be prepared to throw it out and start again!

Action Planning

A great way to get some action during the What's Next? Is to create an action plan. Spend some time now putting down some actions you can get started on immediately. You are probably very familiar with SMART Action goals (Specific, Measurable, Achievable, Realistic and Timely). Here I've put a bit of a twist on this. Design Thinking now becomes integral to the process. You can draw this up on a whiteboard and have a go yourself. Go ahead be creative! Perhaps you might even use colorful visualizations like Mind Mapping to create your business goals. But just remember; don't become overly attached to your goals. This only defeats the purpose of being flexible and adaptable. Yes we must have goals but we also need to find a middle way between, strict adherence to our goals and being able to throw them out quickly if we need to. Instead, try to maintain a focus on the original intentions behind your goals.

Design Action	Everyone's Responsible	Deadline	Resources	Stop the Change Challengers	Result
What Design Thinking task will be done?	*What great people will be involved?*	*By when? Lets get started*	*What do you need to complete this step? Fail Fast and Cheap!!*	*But What if it Worked?*	*Dream the future*
What is?					
What if?					
What Works?					
What Wows?					

Right on Target!

Using Design Thinking for more than just Innovation.

Contemporary discourse in Design Thinking for Business looks at its uses for innovation. However, the tools of Design can help us do more than just innovate. Design Thinking creates a mindset that opens up many possibilities in business. In business we do a lot of planning which is essential for running a profitable company. Our traditional strategic planning process goes something like this: Firstly we look at what we have to offer or our products or services. Then we look at our finances and how much money we have. The third stage usually involves looking at who will be our customers, their locations, their demographics, how much they earn etc. After this we look at what markets we might enter and then spend some time on looking at if we have the key people with the right skills to build, develop or run our product or service. Technology often comes next. We decide what technology we need to build and operate. Then we look at our product capability and finally we set ourselves some clear goals and go off on our merry way to hire new people, purchase our technology and develop our products or services. Sometimes we hit the jackpot with our customers, but most often, and after hiring the wrong people, we completely miss the mark. But hey, we planned this so well and we have endless spreadsheets to prove it! Sound familiar?

The traditional strategic planning process is highly company focussed. What do we want to sell? Our customers will love it, because we are very smart and know what they need. However, as we have seen, when we use or repertoire of Design Thinking tools and skills in the Strategic Planning process we can come up with totally new propositions, that meet our customer's needs and can create a whole new customer base and new markets. Who knows you may disrupt your whole business model?

The tools of Design Thinking now extend way beyond innovation into our everyday business. By using a mix of traditional business tools with modern thinking and tools your business will become resilient to change and position itself at the forefront of your industry. Here's some ways that you can enhance your business processes:

- **Modern Thinking and Traditional ways of looking at our analysis and planning**

Use the tools of the What Is? to analyse the current state of your business. What is? allows us to look at ourselves and our competitors without the limitations of the traditional SWOT. It provides us the opportunity to do this with a customer-centric viewpoint.

- **Business Strategy**

Use all of the tools in your development of your business strategy design. Who knows you may disrupt your whole business model?

- **Business Planning**

The tools of Design Thinking not only help you in your business planning process but when used in conjunction with modern planning techniques such as the Business Canvass Model, it can help you to create a highly resilient business ready to disrupt industries.

- **Value Propositions**

Design Thinking is a marvellously creative way to come up with your business' value propositions. By taking potential customer's needs, fears and risks into account we can create new value propositions. Try using the Serviette Brainstorm to come up with some new value propositions.

- **Sales and Marketing**

The tools of Design help us create amazing marketing and sales programs. Customer Co-creation is central to achieving powerful campaigns.

Our marketing teams are used to using focus groups to source information on our customer needs. However, the traditional modes of focus group testing do not provide insight into the context of everyday life. Using the tools of design such as Ethnography, in the marketing process helps us to determine the difference between what people say they want and what they actually end up doing. Customer Journey Mapping and Customer Co-creation are also powerful tools to use in the development of your marketing strategy and sales campaigns.

- **Tenders**

The use of Design Thinking methodology when planning to write tenders provides your business the competitive edge in the process with the ability to look at what your customer wants and being able to deliver them innovative solutions. My experience in writing successful tenders has shown me that by viewing the current state of play and looking opportunities for innovations for our customer through the use of Design Thinking methodology, results in your tender standing out from the crowd. I have actually used a Customer Journey Map as a visual in a recent winning tender.

- **Continuous Improvement**

The Design Thinking process is one of continuous improvement. It has a natural feedback loop that fits well within Quality Management Systems and allows them to become much more flexible and adaptable than ever before. Customer-centrism and co-creation activities enable improvement with knowledge of our customer needs. Done well, Continuous Improvement becomes Continuous Innovation.

- **Change Management**

We have looked at how change is constant in the modern world and that we need a new discourse in change and make it our ally. Using the tools of Design Thinking provides us with a wonderful method to manage change within our organisations. Using a collaborative approach to problem solving and involving a diverse group of staff throughout the process helps to get buy in from even the most reluctant. Those most reluctant to change have been part of the solution.

- **Making Meetings Mean Something (not just meetings about meetings, for the**

sake of meetings)

By using Design Thinking methods for the basis of your meetings, each event will become meaningful and an opportunity for collaboration and new ideas. Next time you schedule a meeting you might want to pose a problem to those who are attending and hand out some paper serviettes and a voucher for a coffee, for them to brainstorm ideas before coming along.

Create a structure for your meeting that makes time for new ideas to be looked at. Make sure you use meetings as platforms to create new ideas for your customer's unmet needs and not just meetings about meetings to schedule more meetings.

- **Recruitment and Human Resources**

Using Design Thinking methodology for recruitment campaigns brings a new light to our HR processes. When combined with the outcomes of your strategy sessions and with your customers seen as central to your strategy design, you can really think about who you hire and how that will help you with your business or new product or service.

Can you think of other ways to weave Design Thinking into your day-to-day business?

What's Next?

Over the course of our journey through the Disruption Code we have looked the threat of constant change to our business and the imperative for incremental and disruptive innovation through the notion of Disrupt or be Disrupted. We've seen some great innovations that have come from Business Model Disruption such as the likes of the iPod, and we have viewed failure as our success and change as our friend. By now we've hopefully stopped the "busyness" that gets in the way of our success.
We've also looked at how we can bring Innovation into our business' DNA through the creation of collaborative workspaces, customer-centrism and extending Design Thinking, and the tools that Designers use into our business framework. We've looked at how using modern thinking hand-in-hand with our tried and true business processes, creates a powerful new paradigm for business success and growth.

You now have the beginning of your repertoire of tools to implement change and innovation into your day-to-day business and enable you to crack the Disruption Code for yourself.

This is the just the beginning of your journey to growth, success and creating a resilient and innovative company into the future. So now the What's Next? is indeed **Over to you!**

ABOUT INNNOVATION CREATION

At Innovation Creation and our Innovation Design Institute, we step outside the boundaries and constraints of traditional business to disrupt business models. We use simple and powerful strategies to help you overtake your competitors.

Although 'Design Thinking' is by no means a new phenomenon and has traditionally been used in the world of design; it is fast becoming recognized by businesses across the world as a great tool to disrupt traditional models of business. We work with you to show you how Design Thinking can work hand in hand with traditional business models to create new and exciting products and services for business. 'Design Thinking' becomes a transformative process when a business' leaders drive the process.

Want to learn more about Design Thinking for your business? Need help disrupting your business model, or want help in your next strategy planning event or retreat? Let us help you!

Contact Innovation Creation at
info@innovationcreation.com.au
www.innovationcreation.com.au

Follow us on Twitter®   @innovatcreation

Or find us on Facebook® or Google®

ABOUT THE AUTHOR

Julie Beckers, Principal of Innovation Creation, is a highly acclaimed senior executive with over 20 years of business development experience. Throughout her working career Julie has demonstrated a great deal of passion for her work which is substantiated by her numerous successes. Her skills in business development have assisted her in taking corporations from million dollar turnovers to multimillion-dollar turnovers, in addition to increasing their market share by 50%. As a highly creative influencer, Julie's recent successes include writing an innovative tender for a company that attained a $30M contract, an accomplishment of which Julie is extremely proud. Julie is well known for her ability to step outside the traditional constraints of business models to provide Disruptive Innovation and specializes in providing companies with powerful strategies that enable them to overtake competitors.

www.ingramcontent.com/pod-product-compliance
Lightning Source LLC
Chambersburg PA
CBHW070901180526
45168CB00005B/1897